Put Me in the Zoo

A guide for the book by Robert Lopshire
Great Works Author: Tracy Pearce

Image Credits

Cover, pp. 11–12, 14, 21, 24, 32–33, 54, 69–70 Shutterstock; pp. 20, 22, 59–61 Timothy J. Bradley.

Standards

© 2007 Teachers of English to Speakers of Other Languages, Inc. (TESOL)
© 2007 Board of Regents of the University of Wisconsin System. World-Class Instructional Design and Assessment (WIDA)
© Copyright 2010. National Governors Association Center for Best Practices and Council of Chief State School Officers.
All rights reserved.

Shell Education
5301 Oceanus Drive
Huntington Beach, CA 92649-1030
http://www.shelleducation.com
ISBN 978-1-4258-8962-3
© 2015 Shell Educational Publishing, Inc.

The classroom teacher may reproduce copies of materials in this book for classroom use only. The reproduction of any part for an entire school or school system is strictly prohibited. No part of this publication may be transmitted, stored, or recorded in any form without written permission from the publisher.

Table of contents

How to Use This Literature Guide 4
    Theme Thoughts 4
    Vocabulary 5
    Analyzing the Literature 6
    Reader Response 6
    Guided Close Reading 6
    Making Connections 7
    Language Learning 7
    Story Elements 7
    Culminating Activity 8
    Comprehension Assessment 8
    Response to Literature 8

Correlation to the Standards 8
    Purpose and Intent of Standards 8
    How to Find Standards Correlations 8
    Standards Correlation Chart 9
    TESOL and WIDA Standards 10

About the Author—Robert Lopshire 11
    Possible Texts for Text Comparisons 11

Book Summary of *Put Me in the Zoo* 12
    Cross-Curricular Connection 12
    Possible Texts for Text Sets 12

Teacher Plans and Student Pages 13
    Pre-Reading Theme Thoughts 13
    Section 1: Pages 1–23 15
    Section 2: Pages 24–35 27
    Section 3: Pages 36–47 37
    Section 4: Pages 48–61 48

Post-Reading Activities 57
    Post-Reading Theme Thoughts 57
    Culminating Activity: The Zoo and the Circus 58
    Comprehension Assessment 64
    Response to Literature: The Leopard and His Spots 66

Writing Paper 69

Answer Key 71

Introduction

How to Use This Literature Guide

Today's standards demand rigor and relevance in the reading of complex texts. The units in this series guide teachers in a rich and deep exploration of worthwhile works of literature for classroom study. The most rigorous instruction can also be interesting and engaging!

Many current strategies for effective literacy instruction have been incorporated into these instructional guides for literature. Throughout the units, text-dependent questions are used to determine comprehension of the book as well as student interpretation of the vocabulary words. The books chosen for the series are complex and are exemplars of carefully crafted works of literature. Close reading is used throughout the units to guide students toward revisiting the text and using textual evidence to respond to prompts orally and in writing. Students must analyze the story elements in multiple assignments for each section of the book. All of these strategies work together to rigorously guide students through their study of literature.

The next few pages describe how to use this guide for a purposeful and meaningful literature study. Each section of this guide is set up in the same way to make it easier for you to implement the instruction in your classroom.

Theme Thoughts

The great works of literature used throughout this series have important themes that have been relevant to people for many years. Many of the themes will be discussed during the various sections of this instructional guide. However, it would also benefit students to have independent time to think about the key themes of the book.

Before students begin reading, have them complete the *Pre-Reading Theme Thoughts* (page 13). This graphic organizer will allow students to think about the themes outside the context of the story. They'll have the opportunity to evaluate statements based on important themes and defend their opinions. Be sure to keep students' papers for comparison to the *Post-Reading Theme Thoughts* (page 57). This graphic organizer is similar to the pre-reading activity. However, this time, students will be answering the questions from the point of view of one of the characters in the book. They have to think about how the character would feel about each statement and defend their thoughts. To conclude the activity, have students compare what they thought about the themes before they read the book to what the characters discovered during the story.

Introduction

How to Use This Literature Guide (cont.)

Vocabulary

Each teacher reference vocabulary overview page has definitions and sentences about how key vocabulary words are used in the section. These words should be introduced and discussed with students. Students will use these words in different activities throughout the book.

On some of the vocabulary student pages, students are asked to answer text-related questions about vocabulary words from the sections. The following question stems will help you create your own vocabulary questions if you'd like to extend the discussion.

- How does this word describe _____'s character?
- How does this word connect to the problem in this story?
- How does this word help you understand the setting?
- Tell me how this word connects to the main idea of this story.
- What visual pictures does this word bring to your mind?
- Why do you think the author used this word?

At times, you may find that more work with the words will help students understand their meanings and importance. These quick vocabulary activities are a good way to further study the words.

- Students can play vocabulary concentration. Make one set of cards that has the words on them and another set with the definitions. Then, have students lay them out on the table and play concentration. The goal of the game is to match vocabulary words with their definitions. For early readers or English language learners, the two sets of cards could be the words and pictures of the words.

- Students can create word journal entries about the words. Students choose words they think are important and then describe why they think each word is important within the book. Early readers or English language learners could instead draw pictures about the words in a journal.

- Students can create puppets and use them to act out the vocabulary words from the stories. Students may also enjoy telling their own character-driven stories using vocabulary words from the original stories.

Introduction

How to Use This Literature Guide (cont.)

Analyzing the Literature

After you have read each section with students, hold a small-group or whole-class discussion. Provided on the teacher reference page for each section are leveled questions. The questions are written at two levels of complexity to allow you to decide which questions best meet the needs of your students. The Level 1 questions are typically less abstract than the Level 2 questions. These questions are focused on the various story elements, such as character, setting, and plot. Be sure to add further questions as your students discuss what they've read. For each question, a few key points are provided for your reference as you discuss the book with students.

Reader Response

In today's classrooms, there are often great readers who are below average writers. So much time and energy is spent in classrooms getting students to read on grade level that little time is left to focus on writing skills. To help teachers include more writing in their daily literacy instruction, each section of this guide has a literature-based reader response prompt. Each of the three genres of writing is used in the reader responses within this guide: narrative, informative/explanatory, and opinion. Before students write, you may want to allow them time to draw pictures related to the topic. Book-themed writing paper is provided on pages 69–70 if your students need more space to write.

Guided Close Reading

Within each section of this guide, it is suggested that you closely reread a portion of the text with your students. Page numbers are given, but since some versions of the books may have different page numbers, the sections to be reread are described by location as well. After rereading the section, there are a few text-dependent questions to be answered by students.

Working space has been provided to help students prepare for the group discussion. They should record their thoughts and ideas on the activity page and refer to it during your discussion. Rather than just taking notes, you may want to require students to write complete responses to the questions before discussing them with you.

Encourage students to read one question at a time and then go back to the text and discover the answer. Work with students to ensure that they use the text to determine their answers rather than making unsupported inferences. Suggested answers are provided in the answer key.

How to Use This Literature Guide (cont.)

Guided Close Reading (cont.)

The generic open-ended stems below can be used to write your own text-dependent questions if you would like to give students more practice.

- What words in the story support . . . ?
- What text helps you understand . . . ?
- Use the book to tell why _____ happens.
- Based on the events in the story, . . . ?
- Show me the part in the text that supports . . . .
- Use the text to tell why . . . .

Making Connections

The activities in this section help students make cross-curricular connections to mathematics, science, social studies, fine arts, or other curricular areas. These activities require higher-order thinking skills from students but also allow for creative thinking.

Language Learning

A special section has been set aside to connect the literature to language conventions. Through these activities, students will have opportunities to practice the conventions of standard English grammar, usage, capitalization, and punctuation.

Story Elements

It is important to spend time discussing what the common story elements are in literature. Understanding the characters, setting, plot, and theme can increase students' comprehension and appreciation of the story. If teachers begin discussing these elements in early childhood, students will more likely internalize the concepts and look for the elements in their independent reading. Another very important reason for focusing on the story elements is that students will be better writers if they think about how the stories they read are constructed.

In the story elements activities, students are asked to create work related to the characters, setting, or plot. Consider having students complete only one of these activities. If you give students a choice on this assignment, each student can decide to complete the activity that most appeals to him or her. Different intelligences are used so that the activities are diverse and interesting to all students.

How to Use This Literature Guide (cont.)

Culminating Activity

At the end of this instructional guide is a creative culminating activity that allows students the opportunity to share what they've learned from reading the book. This activity is open ended so that students can push themselves to create their own great works within your language arts classroom.

Comprehension Assessment

The questions in this section require students to think about the book they've read as well as the words that were used in the book. Some questions are tied to quotations from the book to engage students and require them to think about the text as they answer the questions.

Response to Literature

Finally, students are asked to respond to the literature by drawing pictures and writing about the characters and stories. A suggested rubric is provided for teacher reference.

Correlation to the Standards

Shell Education is committed to producing educational materials that are research and standards based. As part of this effort, we have correlated all of our products to the academic standards of all 50 states, the District of Columbia, the Department of Defense Dependents Schools, and all Canadian provinces.

Purpose and Intent of Standards

Standards are designed to focus instruction and guide adoption of curricula. Standards are statements that describe the criteria necessary for students to meet specific academic goals. They define the knowledge, skills, and content students should acquire at each level. Standards are also used to develop standardized tests to evaluate students' academic progress. Teachers are required to demonstrate how their lessons meet standards. Standards are used in the development of all of our products, so educators can be assured they meet high academic standards.

How to Find Standards Correlations

To print a customized correlation report of this product for your state, visit our website at http://www.shelleducation.com and follow the online directions. If you require assistance in printing correlation reports, please contact our Customer Service Department at 1-877-777-3450.

Correlation to the Standards (cont.)

Standards Correlation Chart

The lessons in this book were written to support the Common Core College and Career Readiness Anchor Standards. The following chart indicates which lessons address the anchor standards.

Common Core College and Career Readiness Anchor Standard	Section
CCSS.ELA-Literacy.CCRA.R.1—Read closely to determine what the text says explicitly and to make logical inferences from it; cite specific textual evidence when writing or speaking to support conclusions drawn from the text.	Analyzing the Literature Sections 1–4; Guided Close Reading Sections 1–4; Story Elements Sections 1–4
CCSS.ELA-Literacy.CCRA.R.2—Determine central ideas or themes of a text and analyze their development; summarize the key supporting details and ideas.	Analyzing the Literature Sections 1–4; Guided Close Reading Sections 1–4; Post-Reading Response to Literature
CCSS.ELA-Literacy.CCRA.R.3—Analyze how and why individuals, events, or ideas develop and interact over the course of a text.	Analyzing the Literature Sections 1–4; Guided Close Reading Sections 1–4; Story Elements Sections 1–4; Post-Reading Response to Literature
CCSS.ELA-Literacy.CCRA.R.4—Interpret words and phrases as they are used in a text, including determining technical, connotative, and figurative meanings, and analyze how specific word choices shape meaning or tone.	Vocabulary Sections 1–4; Analyzing the Literature Sections 1–4
CCSS.ELA-Literacy.CCRA.W.1—Write arguments to support claims in an analysis of substantive topics or texts using valid reasoning and relevant and sufficient evidence.	Reader Response Sections 2, 4
CCSS.ELA-Literacy.CCRA.W.2—Write informative/explanatory texts to examine and convey complex ideas and information clearly and accurately through the effective selection, organization, and analysis of content.	Reader Response Section 3
CCSS.ELA-Literacy.CCRA.W.3—Write narratives to develop real or imagined experiences or events using effective technique, well-chosen details and well-structured event sequences.	Reader Response Section 1
CCSS.ELA-Literacy.CCRA.W.4—Produce clear and coherent writing in which the development, organization, and style are appropriate to task, purpose, and audience.	Reader Response Sections 1–4; Culminating Activity
CCSS.ELA-Literacy.CCRA.W.6—Use technology, including the Internet, to produce and publish writing and to interact and collaborate with others.	Culminating Activity

Introduction

Correlation to the Standards (cont.)

Standards Correlation Chart (cont.)

Common Core College and Career Readiness Anchor Standard	Section
CCSS.ELA-Literacy.CCRA.L.1—Demonstrate command of the conventions of standard English grammar and usage when writing or speaking.	Reader Response Sections 1–4; Language Learning Sections 1–4; Story Elements Sections 1–4
CCSS.ELA-Literacy.CCRA.L.3—Apply knowledge of language to understand how language functions in different contexts, to make effective choices for meaning or style, and to comprehend more fully when reading or listening.	Analyzing the Literature Sections 1–4; Guided Close Reading Sections 1–4; Language Learning Sections 1–4
CCSS.ELA-Literacy.CCRA.L.4—Determine or clarify the meaning of unknown and multiple-meaning words and phrases by using context clues, analyzing meaningful word parts, and consulting general and specialized reference materials, as appropriate.	Vocabulary Sections 1–4
CCSS.ELA-Literacy.CCRA.L.5—Demonstrate understanding of figurative language, word relationships, and nuances in word meanings.	Making Connections Sections 1–4
CCSS.ELA-Literacy.CCRA.L.6—Acquire and use accurately a range of general academic and domain-specific words and phrases sufficient for reading, writing, speaking, and listening at the college and career readiness level; demonstrate independence in gathering vocabulary knowledge when encountering an unknown term important to comprehension or expression.	Vocabulary Sections 1–4; Story Elements Sections 1–4; Culminating Activity

TESOL and WIDA Standards

The lessons in this book promote English language development for English language learners. The following TESOL and WIDA English Language Development Standards are addressed through the activities in this book:

- **Standard 1:** English language learners communicate for social and instructional purposes within the school setting.
- **Standard 2:** English language learners communicate information, ideas and concepts necessary for academic success in the content area of language arts.

About the Author—Robert Lopshire

Robert Lopshire was born on April 14, 1927, in Sarasota, Florida. He obtained his pilot's license by the age of 15. After graduating from Sarasota High School in 1944, he served in the military during World War II aboard assault landing ships in the Pacific Theater.

When the war ended, Lopshire worked as an illustrator in Boston and Philadelphia. He became a member of the Illustrators Group in New York. He received many painting awards for his realistic still lifes and landscapes.

Lopshire began his writing career when he was the creative arts director during the early years of the Beginner Books series at Random House. He thought he could write stories that were superior to many of the manuscripts he had to read. His illustrations for *Ann Can Fly*, which was published in 1959, also caught the eye of Dr. Seuss. Since those early years, he wrote and illustrated various best-selling children's books. *Put Me in the Zoo* became a best seller and is part of the Beginner Books series. Lopshire passed away in 2002.

Possible Texts for Text Comparisons

I Want to Be Somebody New!, *New Tricks I Can Do!*, *Put Me in the Alphabet! A Beginner Workbook About ABC's*, and *I Want to Count Something New: A Beginner Workbook About 1,2,3's*, all have Spot as a character in the story and could be used for enriching text comparisons by the same author. *I Am Better Than You!*, also written by Robert Lopshire, could be used as a text comparison that focuses on being happy with yourself or the concept that everyone is special in his or her own way.

Introduction

Book Summary of *Put Me in the Zoo*

This book is the first in a series that features Spot, a spotted leopard. Spot truly believes he belongs in the zoo. Throughout the story, Spot shows his two young human friends how he can change his spots and colors in an attempt to gain admittance to the zoo. Spot demonstrates many silly antics including juggling his own spots, moving his spots all around, and changing the size of his spots. He does all of this to show his two friends that he is special enough to be exhibited in the zoo. At the very end, Spot discovers he really is extraordinary and belongs in a circus rather than the zoo.

Cross-Curricular Connection

This book can be used in a social science unit on how everyone is special in their own ways or a science unit on zoos.

Possible Texts for Text Sets

- Candlewick Press. *Peppa Pig and the Busy Day at School*. Candlewick, 2013.
- Cocca-Leffler, Maryann. *Jack's Talent*. Farrar, Straus and Giroux, 2007.
- Fearnley, Jan. *Just Like You*. Candlewick, 2001.
- Kates, Bobbi. *We're Different, We're the Same (Sesame Street)*. Random House Books for Young Readers, 1992.
- Okerfelt, Suzanne Tonner. *You are Unique*. CreateSpace Independent Publishing Platform, 2013.

or

- Bostrom, Kathleen Long. *The View at the Zoo*. Ideals Children's Books, 2011.
- Paxton, Tom. *Going to the Zoo*. HarperCollins, 1996.
- Pfloog, Jan. *The Zoo Book*. Golden Books, 1999.
- Rey, Margret, and H.A. Rey. *Curious George Visits the Zoo*. HMH Books for Young Readers, 1985.
- Wildsmith, Brian. *Zoo Animals*. Starbright Books, 2002.

Name _____   Introduction

Pre-Reading Theme Thoughts

Directions: Draw a picture of a happy face or a sad face. Your face should show how you feel about each statement. Then, use words to say what you think about each statement.

Statement	How Do You Feel? 😊 ☹	Why Do You Feel This Way?
It is okay to be different.		
Everyone is special in his or her own way.		
Things come in all shapes and sizes.		
You can find where you belong.		

Teacher Plans—Pre-Reading

Discussion and Activities

Previewing the Cover

1. Display the cover of *Put Me in the Zoo*. Read aloud the title and the author's name. Explain that the author in this book also illustrated the pictures.
2. Explain that good readers make predictions before, during, and after reading. Tell students that a prediction is making a guess about what will happen or what something will be about.
3. In pairs, have students share their predictions about the book based on the title and the images from the cover.

Previewing the Book

1. Take a picture walk through the book to allow students to look at all the illustrations. Pause at various points in the book to discuss what students' have seen and to allow them to make predictions.
2. Based on the picture walk, ask students to identify if the book is fiction or nonfiction and how they know.
3. Tell students that there are three main characters in this book. There is the leopard, the boy, and the girl.
4. Have students talk to each other about what they think the leopard, the boy, and the girl are going to do in this story.

Teacher Plans—Section 1
Pages 1-23

Vocabulary Overview

Key words and phrases from this section are provided below with definitions and sentences about how the words are used in the story. Introduce and discuss these important vocabulary words with students. If you think these words or other words in the story warrant more time devoted to them, there are suggestions in the introduction for other vocabulary activities.

Word	Definition	Sentence about Text
zoo (p. 3)	a place where many kinds of animals are kept so that people can see them	The leopard is going to the **zoo**.
keep (p. 7)	to continue having or holding something	The leopard wonders if they will **keep** him in the zoo.
stay (p. 9)	to continue to be in the same place for a period of time	The leopard wants to **stay** in the zoo.
should (p. 11)	used to emphasize what is probable or expected	The leopard thinks he **should** be in the zoo.
good (p. 13)	having or showing talent or skill	The kids ask the leopard what **good** things he can do.
spots (p. 15)	small round areas that are a different color from the surface around them	The leopard's **spots** change colors.
violet (p. 21)	a bluish-purple color	All of the leopard's spots are **violet**.
more (p. 21)	extra or additional	The children want the leopard to do **more** tricks.
wish (p. 21)	to want or ask to do something	The children **wish** the leopard would do more.
new (p. 23)	not experienced before	Turning his spots all different colors is a **new** trick.

Name _____

Vocabulary Activity

Directions: Draw lines to complete the sentences.

Beginnings of Sentences

After green, he made

All his **spots**

What **new** tricks

Will they **keep**

I want to

Endings of Sentences

me in the **zoo**?

will he do next?

are blue!

stay in the **zoo**.

his spots **violet**.

Directions: Answer this question.

1. What do the children want **more** of?
_____
_____
_____
_____

Teacher Plans—Section 1
Pages 1-23

Analyzing the Literature

Provided below are discussion questions you can use in small groups, with the whole class, or for written assignments. Each question is written at two levels so you can choose the right question for each group of students. For each question, a few key points are provided for your reference as you discuss the book with students.

Story Element	Level 1	Level 2	Key Discussion Points
Character	Who are the characters in the story?	Describe how each character is introduced in the story.	The characters are a leopard, the zookeepers, a boy, and a girl. The leopard is introduced when he walks into the zoo. The zookeepers are working at the zoo. The boy and girl are shown when the leopard is asking the zookeepers to stay in the zoo.
Setting	What is the setting of the story?	Describe what is important about the setting of the story.	The story takes place inside the zoo and in front of the entrance of the zoo. Students should use the illustrations to gather information about the setting. The setting is important because the zoo is where the leopard wants to be.
Plot	What is the problem in the story?	Describe the problem in the story, and predict what you think will happen next.	The problem is that the leopard wants to stay in the zoo. The zookeepers do not want him to stay, and they make him leave. The leopard is very sad and tries to prove that he is special. Students' predictions will vary, but they should be based on the text.
Plot	What things does the leopard show the children?	Why does the leopard start doing tricks for the children?	First, the leopard shows the children blue spots. Then, he changes the color of his spots to green and violet. Finally, his spots change to many colors at one time. He is doing tricks to show the children why he should be allowed to stay in the zoo.

© Shell Education #40007—Instructional Guide: Put Me in the Zoo

Pages 1–23

Name _____

Reader Response

Think

Think about a time you have gone to the zoo. If you have not gone to a zoo before, think about animals that might live in a zoo.

Narrative Writing Prompt

Write about what life is like for animals that live at zoos. Tell about the different animals and what they do at the zoo.

Name _____

Pages 1-23

Guided close Reading

Closely reread when the children ask why the leopard should be in the zoo (pages 13–15).

Directions: Think about these questions. In the space below, write ideas or draw pictures as you think. Be ready to share your answers.

❶ Looking back at the book, what questions do the children ask the leopard?

❷ Using the text and the pictures, what is the first trick the leopard does?

❸ What do the illustrations tell us about how the leopard feels?

© Shell Education　　　　　#40007—Instructional Guide: Put Me in the Zoo　　19

Making connections—changing colors

Directions: The leopard changes the color of his spots. There are some animals that can change their colors to help them survive. Draw a habitat for each animal below. Then, color your picture so the animal blends in with its home.

chameleon

arctic fox

mimic octopus

Peron's tree frog

Name _____

Pages 1-23

Making connections—colors

Directions: The leopard changes his spots to many different colors. Look at the pictures below. Color the boxes that have violet items violet. Color the boxes that have green items green. Color the boxes that have yellow items yellow.

grapes	chick	shamrock
grass	plum	corn
cheese	jelly	frog

© Shell Education

#40007—Instructional Guide: Put Me in the Zoo

21

Making connections—Spotty Pattern

Directions: The leopard has spots with many colors. Make a spotty pattern on the leopard below. You can use dot markers, circles from a hole punch, or a pencil eraser dipped in paint or an inkpad to make your spots.

Name _____

Pages 1-23

Language Learning—The -oo Sound

Directions: Fill in the missing -oo digraph. Read each word and then draw a picture to match the word.

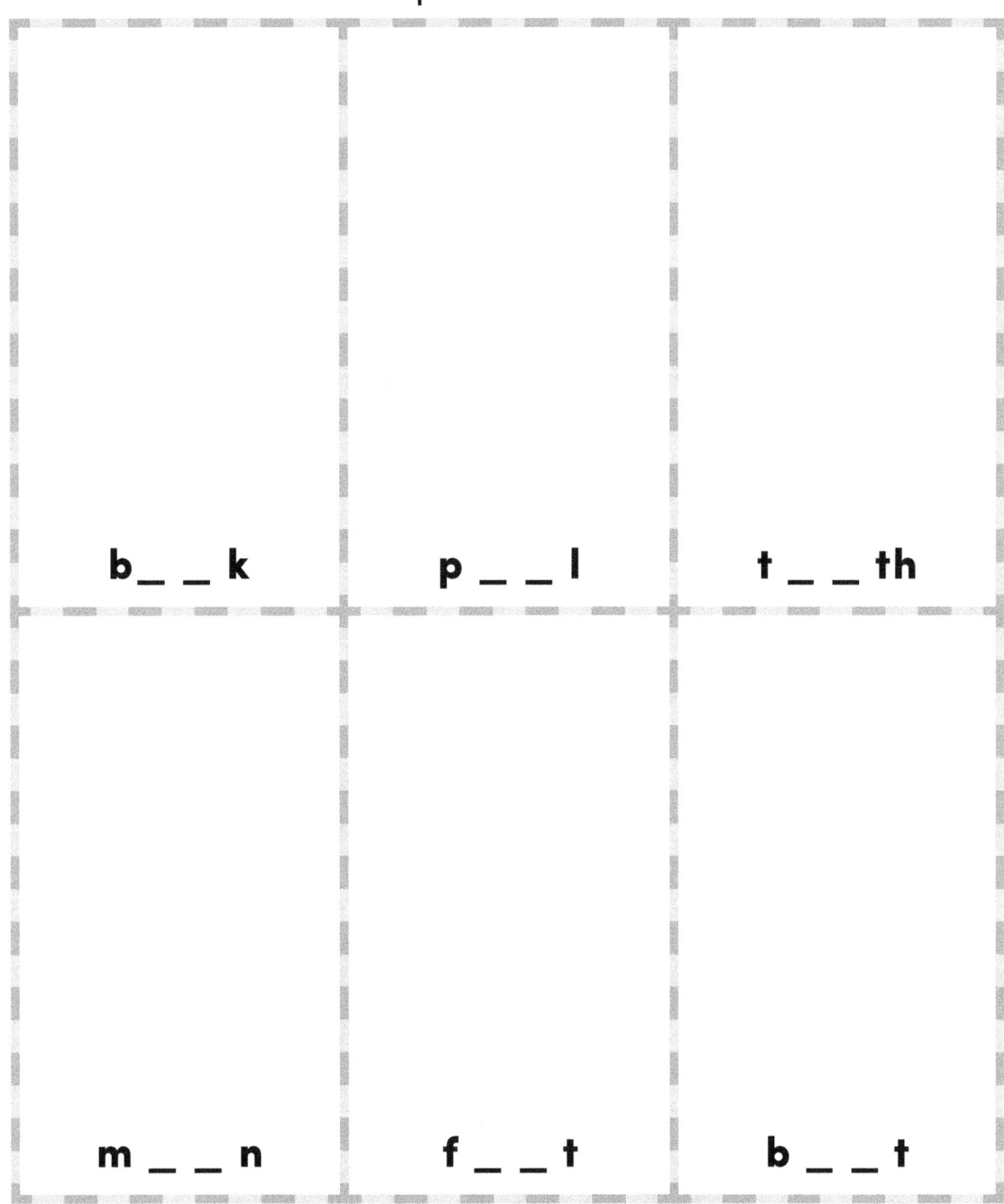

b _ _ k

p _ _ l

t _ _ th

m _ _ n

f _ _ t

b _ _ t

Pages 1-23

Name _____

Story Elements—Setting

Directions: Complete the poem to describe the setting of this section in the book.

_____

I see _____.

_____

I hear _____.

_____

I smell _____.

_____

I feel _____.

_____

I taste _____.

Name _____

Pages 1-23

Story Elements—Character

Directions: Draw the leopard's face to show how the leopard is feeling in each section described below.

I want to stay in the zoo.	Out you go from the zoo!
I can make green spots!	"Do more!"

© Shell Education   #40007—Instructional Guide: Put Me in the Zoo   25

Pages 1–23

Name _____

Story Elements—Plot

Directions: Fill in what happens next.

"I want to stay in here with you." →

_____
_____
_____
_____
_____
_____
_____

• •

"Look! Now all his spots are blue!" →

_____
_____
_____
_____
_____
_____
_____

Teacher Plans—Section 2
Pages 24-35

Vocabulary Overview

Key words and phrases from this section are provided below with definitions and sentences about how the words are used in the story. Introduce and discuss these important vocabulary words with students. If you think these words or other words in the story warrant more time devoted to them, there are suggestions in the introduction for other vocabulary activities.

Word	Definition	Sentence about Text
my (p. 24)	relating to or belonging to me	I put **my** spots on the ball.
up (p. 24)	from a lower to a higher place or position	The leopard put his spots **up** on the ball.
them (p. 25)	used to refer to certain people, animals, or things	The leopard put **them** on the wall.
wall (p. 25)	a structure of brick or stone that surrounds an area or separates one area from another	The leopard put the spots on the **wall**.
cat (p. 27)	a small animal that is related to lions and tigers and is often kept by people as a pet	The leopard put his spots on the **cat**.
hat (p. 27)	covering for the head that often has a brim and a rounded or flat top	The leopard put his spots on the **hat**.
now (p. 30)	in the next moment; very soon	**Now**, look at this!
tree (p. 31)	a usually tall plant that has a thick, wooden stem and many large branches	The leopard put his spots on the **tree**.
back (p. 33)	to or toward a former state or condition	The leopard put his spots **back** on himself!
here (p. 35)	appearing or happening now	**Here** is one more!

Pages 24–35

Name _____

Vocabulary Activity

Directions: Choose at least two words from the story. Draw a picture that shows what these words mean. Label your picture.

Words from the Story

my	up	them	wall	cat
hat	now	tree	back	here

Directions: Answer this question.

1. Where does the leopard put the spots **back** on?
_____
- - - - - - - - - - - -
_____

Analyzing the Literature

Provided below are discussion questions you can use in small groups, with the whole class, or for written assignments. Each question is written at two levels so you can choose the right question for each group of students. For each question, a few key points are provided for your reference as you discuss the book with students.

Story Element	Level 1	Level 2	Key Discussion Points
Setting	Describe the new setting in this section.	What is the importance of the setting change in this section?	The setting changes from in front of the zoo to under a tree. The focus is more on the characters than on the setting of the zoo in this section.
Character	Describe the illustrations of the children in this section.	Looking at the illustrations, describe how the children feel about the leopard's tricks	The children look very amused and seem to like all the tricks the leopard is doing. When the spots are on the children, they look at their clothes. When the spots disappear off of them, they look at their clothes again.
Plot	What other tricks does the leopard show the children?	For what reasons does the leopard show the children different tricks?	The leopard puts his spots on a ball, a wall, a cat, a hat, and on the children. He puts them on a tree and on the count of three puts his spots back on himself. Lastly, he turns his spots into four spots. The leopard wants to show the children that he is special.
Plot	What color are the spots in this section of the story?	Describe the spots in this section of the story.	The spots are red in this section of the story. The spots remain red, but they keep changing locations from the ball to the hat to the tree.

Pages 24-35

Name _____

Reader Response

Think
Think about the leopard and if he should be allowed to stay in the zoo.

Opinion Writing Prompt
Write your opinion on whether or not you think the leopard should be allowed to stay in the zoo. Be sure to include reasons to support your opinion.

Name _____

Pages 24-35

Guided Close Reading

Closely reread the part where the leopard puts his spots back on himself. Stop after he juggles his spots (pages 32–35).

Directions: Think about these questions. In the space below, write ideas or draw pictures as you think. Be ready to share your answers.

❶ What words does the leopard say to get all his spots back on him?

❷ What does he do after he makes his spots into four big spots?

❸ Based on the events of the story, why does the leopard think they should put him in the zoo?

Pages 24-35

Name _____

Making Connections—Find the Rhyme

Directions: Circle the picture that rhymes with the first picture in each row. Write the rhyming word on each line.

 cat	 	
 fall	 	
 rug	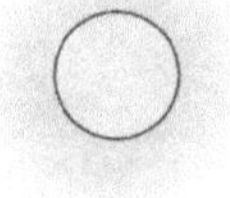 	
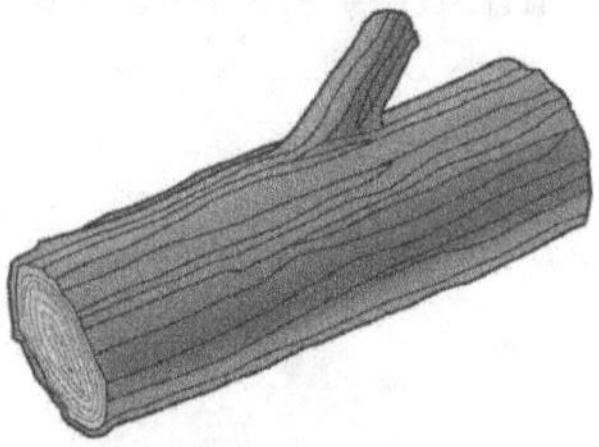 log	 	

Name _____

Pages 24-35

Language Learning— Exclamations Are Fun!

Directions: Exclamation points show the reader that the words are exciting. Write at least three sentences about this section of the story. Each one must end with an exclamation point.

Pages 24-35

Name _____

Story Elements—Setting

Directions: The spots are in many different places in this story. Draw pictures of where the leopard puts his spots. Label each of your pictures.

Name _____

Pages 24-35

Story Elements—Plot

Directions: The events in a story are part of the plot. Match each sequence word with the correct event from this part of the story.

First

Second

Then

Next

Lastly

I put my spots on a hat.

I make four spots.

I put my spots on you!

I put my spots on this ball.

I put my spots on a wall.

Pages 24–35

Name _____

Story Elements—Character

Directions: Choose one of the characters from the story. Write a poem about that character.

_____
_____
_____
_____
_____
_____
_____
_____
_____
_____
_____
_____
_____
_____
_____
_____

Teacher Plans—Section 3
Pages 36-47

Vocabulary Overview

Key words and phrases from this section are provided below with definitions and sentences about how the words are used in the story. Introduce and discuss these important vocabulary words with students. If you think these words or other words in the story warrant more time devoted to them, there are suggestions in the introduction for other vocabulary activities.

Word	Definition	Sentence about Text
take (p. 36)	to carry or move something to a place	The leopard **takes** all his spots.
very (p. 37)	used to emphasize something	The leopard makes his spots **very** small and **very** tall.
small (p. 37)	little in size	The leopard makes his spots very **small**.
tall (p. 39)	greater in height than average	The leopard makes his spots very **tall**.
when (p. 41)	at a specific time	**When** the leopard wants to have fun, he makes his spots all into one big spot.
have (p. 41)	to experience something	The leopard likes to **have** fun with his spots.
fun (p. 41)	enjoyable	Playing with his spots is **fun** for the leopard.
box (p. 44)	a three-dimensional container that has four straight sides, a top, and a bottom	The leopard puts his spots in a **box**.
look (p. 46)	to be something based on appearance	The spots **look** like socks when he takes them out of the box.
socks (p. 46)	clothing worn on the foot	The spots look like **socks**.

Vocabulary Activity

Directions: Complete each sentence below. Use one of the words listed.

Words from the Story

take	very	socks
box	fun	look

1. I _____ all my spots.

2. I want to have more _____.

3. I can put my spots in a _____.

4. The spots _____ like _____.

Directions: Answer this question.

5. What does the leopard make **small** and **tall**?

Teacher Plans—Section 3
Pages 36-47

Analyzing the Literature

Provided below are discussion questions you can use in small groups, with the whole class, or for written assignments. Each question is written at two levels so you can choose the right question for each group of students. For each question, a few key points are provided for your reference as you discuss the book with students.

Story Element	Level 1	Level 2	Key Discussion Points
Plot	What things does the leopard show the children?	Describe how the leopard's tricks are different from earlier in the book.	The leopard makes the spots small and tall. He makes them one spot. He puts them in a box and makes them look like socks. This is different from earlier because before he just changed the color and location. Now, he is changing the size and how the spots are connected to each other.
Setting	Look closely at the illustrations. What do you see in the setting of this section?	Describe the setting of this section and how it compares to the rest of the book.	You can see that the characters are still near the zoo because there are signs that say *zoo*. The signs are slightly different, but they all have an arrow pointing one way. There are also trees, flowers, and bushes in the pictures.
Character	Why does the leopard think he belongs in the zoo?	Why does the leopard keep trying to convince the children that he belongs in the zoo?	The leopard does many things with his spots. He feels he is very special because he can do these great things. He thinks he should be kept in the zoo because he can do those special things with his spots. He refuses to give up, and he hopes that the children will be able to help him.

Pages 36–47

Reader Response

Think

The leopard does many tricks in this story. Think of an animal that you have helped to train or would like to train.

Informative/Explanatory Writing Prompt

Describe what steps you should do to train an animal.

Name _____

Pages 36-47

Guided close Reading

Closely reread where the leopard makes his spots small and tall (pages 36-41).

Directions: Think about these questions. In the space below, write ideas or draw pictures as you think. Be ready to share your answers.

❶ What adjectives does the leopard use to describe the spots?

❷ What words rhyme on these pages?

❸ Look back at the pictures. Is the leopard having fun? Are the children having fun?

Making Connections—Size, Size, Size

Directions: The spots change sizes. The leopard makes them small and tall. Draw spots in each box to show the differences in size.

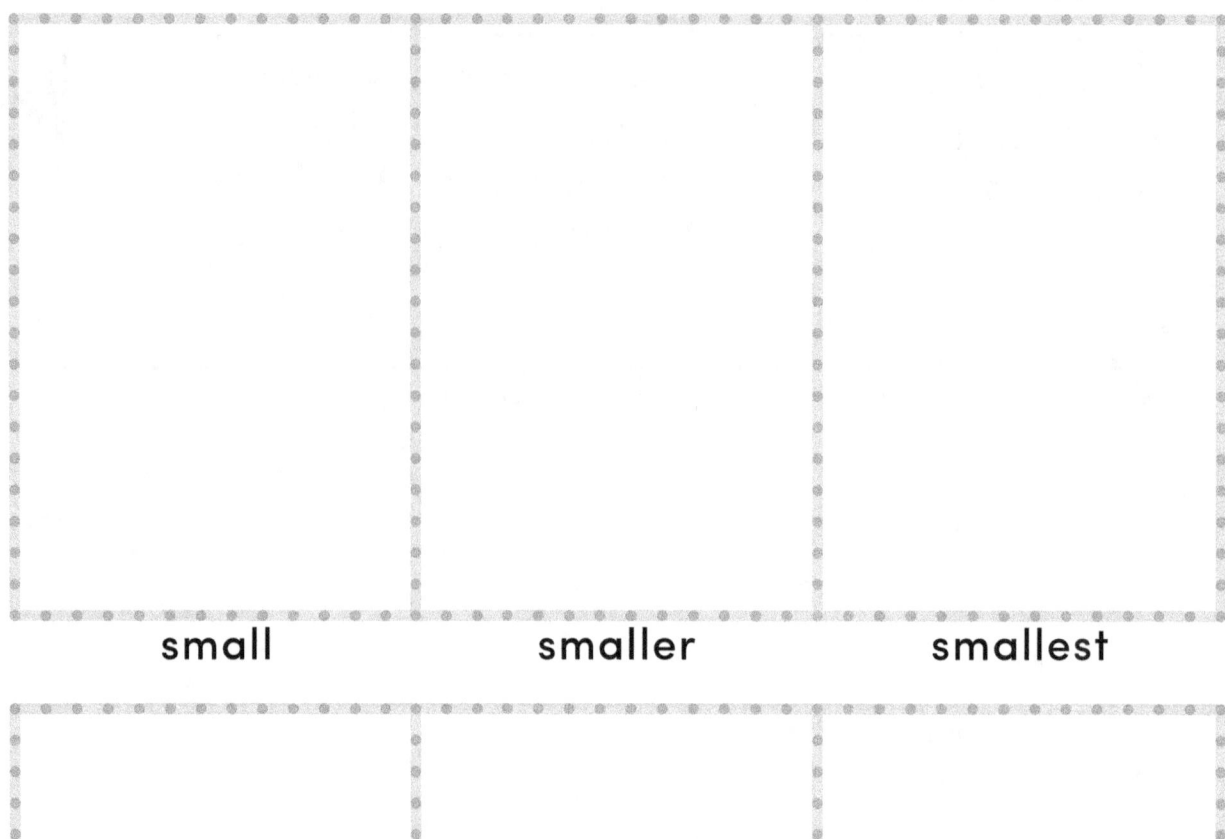

| small | smaller | smallest |

| tall | taller | tallest |

Name _____

Pages 36-47

Making connections—opposite Fun with Antonyms

The leopard turns the spots into different sizes. He makes them small and tall. Tall and small are opposites. Another word for opposite is an *antonym*.

Directions: Look at the words below. Write the antonym or opposite word that goes with each one.

1. **Out** is opposite of _____.

2. **Noisy** is opposite of _____.

3. **Cold** is opposite of _____.

4. **Down** is opposite of _____.

Directions: Write a sentence using a pair of antonyms from above.

_____
_____
_____

Language Learning—Adjectives

Directions: The spots change colors, size, and number. Cut apart the words below. Sort them into the columns.

big	blue	four	green	two
one	red	small	tall	three

Color	Size	Number

Name _____

Pages 36-47

Story Elements—Setting

Directions: Create a three-dimensional image that shows the leopard putting his spots in a box. Think of clever ways to create the leopard and the box so that they are not flat. Can you make those items stand up off this paper?

Pages 36–47   Name _____

Story Elements—Plot

Directions: Cut apart the cards below. Glue them on another piece of paper in the order they happen in the story.

The leopard makes the spots very tall.	The leopard puts the spots in a box.
The spots look like socks.	The leopard makes the spots very small.

Name _____

Pages 36-47

Story Elements—Character

Directions: What else can the leopard do with his spots? Draw a picture of something new that the leopard can do. Write words around your picture to describe it.

Teacher Plans—Section 4
Pages 48–61

Vocabulary Overview

Key words and phrases from this section are provided below with definitions and sentences about how the words are used in the story. Introduce and discuss these important vocabulary words with students. If you think these words or other words in the story warrant more time devoted to them, there are suggestions in the introduction for other vocabulary activities.

Word	Definition	Sentence about Text
way (p. 49)	an adverb to emphasize something	The leopard puts the spots **way** up high.
up (p. 49)	in a high position or place	The leopard puts the spots **up** high.
high (p. 49)	located far above the ground or another surface	The leopard puts the spots **high** above the ground.
fly (p. 49)	to cause something to move through the air	The leopard makes the spots **fly**.
air (p. 51)	the space above the ground that is filled with invisible gases	The leopard puts the spots in the **air**.
call (p. 52)	to speak in a loud voice	The leopard **calls** the spots back.
like (p. 53)	to enjoy something	The leopard asks if the children **like** all the things he can do.
circus (p. 59)	a traveling show that is often performed in a tent; a show that includes trained animals, clowns, and acrobats	The **circus** is the place for the leopard.
place (p. 59)	an appropriate setting	The circus is a good **place** for the leopard.
where (p. 61)	at what location	The circus is **where** the leopard should be.

Name _____

Pages 48-61

Vocabulary Activity

Directions: Practice your writing skills. Write at least two sentences using words from the story.

Words from the Story

way	up	high	fly	air
call	like	circus	place	where

_____

Directions: Answer this question.

1. Why is the **circus** the right **place** for the leopard?
_____

Teacher Plans—Section 4
Pages 48-61

Analyzing the Literature

Provided below are discussion questions you can use in small groups, with the whole class, or for written assignments. Each question is written at two levels so you can choose the right question for each group of students. For each question, a few key points are provided for your reference as you discuss the book with students.

Story Element	Level 1	Level 2	Key Discussion Points
Setting	Describe the setting of this section of the story.	How is the setting of this section of the story different from other sections?	The setting is still by a tree with many spots, but the setting changes at the end with the addition of the circus. The circus is shown with the leopard and the children performing in front of a crowd of people.
Character	How does the leopard feel at the very end of the story?	Describe how the leopard's mood changes throughout the story.	In the beginning of the story, the leopard wants to stay in the zoo, but the zookeepers force him out. The leopard is very upset. The leopard looks very happy at the circus.
Plot	What is the most exciting part of this section of the story?	What is the problem in this story, and how is it solved?	The problem is that the leopard wants to stay in the zoo, but the zookeepers put him out. The leopard does many fancy things with his spots and feels that he should be able to stay in the zoo. The problem is solved when he discovers that the circus is the place for him. The solution is the most exciting part of the story.
Character	How do the children feel about all the things the leopard can do?	Describe how the children feel about the leopard throughout the story.	The children like all of the things that the leopard can do. They like his spots and they like him, as well. They feel he should not be in the zoo, but he should be in the circus.

Name _____

Reader Response

Think

Think about the circus and the zoo. What do you like about each of those places?

Opinion Writing Prompt

Choose whether you would prefer to go to the circus or the zoo. Choose one and give reasons why you would like to go there.

Pages 48-61

Name _____

Guided Close Reading

Closely reread where the leopard and children talk about if he should be in the zoo (pages 54–57).

Directions: Think about these questions. In the space below, write ideas or draw pictures as you think. Be ready to share your answers.

❶ Based on the text, what does the leopard ask the children?

❷ What do the children say to the leopard about the zoo?

❸ Looking back at the pictures, describe the emotions of the little girl on page 57.

Name _____

Pages 48-61

Making connections— Math with Spots

Directions: The leopard changes the number of spots he has. See if you can help the leopard solve these math problems. Draw a picture of each problem. Then, solve each problem.

1. The leopard has 7 yellow spots. He adds 4 blue spots. How many spots does he have all together?

2. The leopard has 12 spots. He makes 6 spots disappear. How many spots does he have left?

3. The leopard makes 9 spots fly in the air. He then makes 5 more spots fly. Oh no, 2 spots fall down. How many spots are flying in the air now?

Pages 48-61

Name _____

Language Learning—Verbs and Nouns

Directions: Read the words from the story below. Color the verbs green and the nouns yellow.

Directions: Choose one verb and one noun from above. Write a sentence.

_____
_____
_____
_____

Name _____

Pages 48–61

Story Elements—Plot

Directions: Sketch four main events from the book. Put them in order using the chart below.

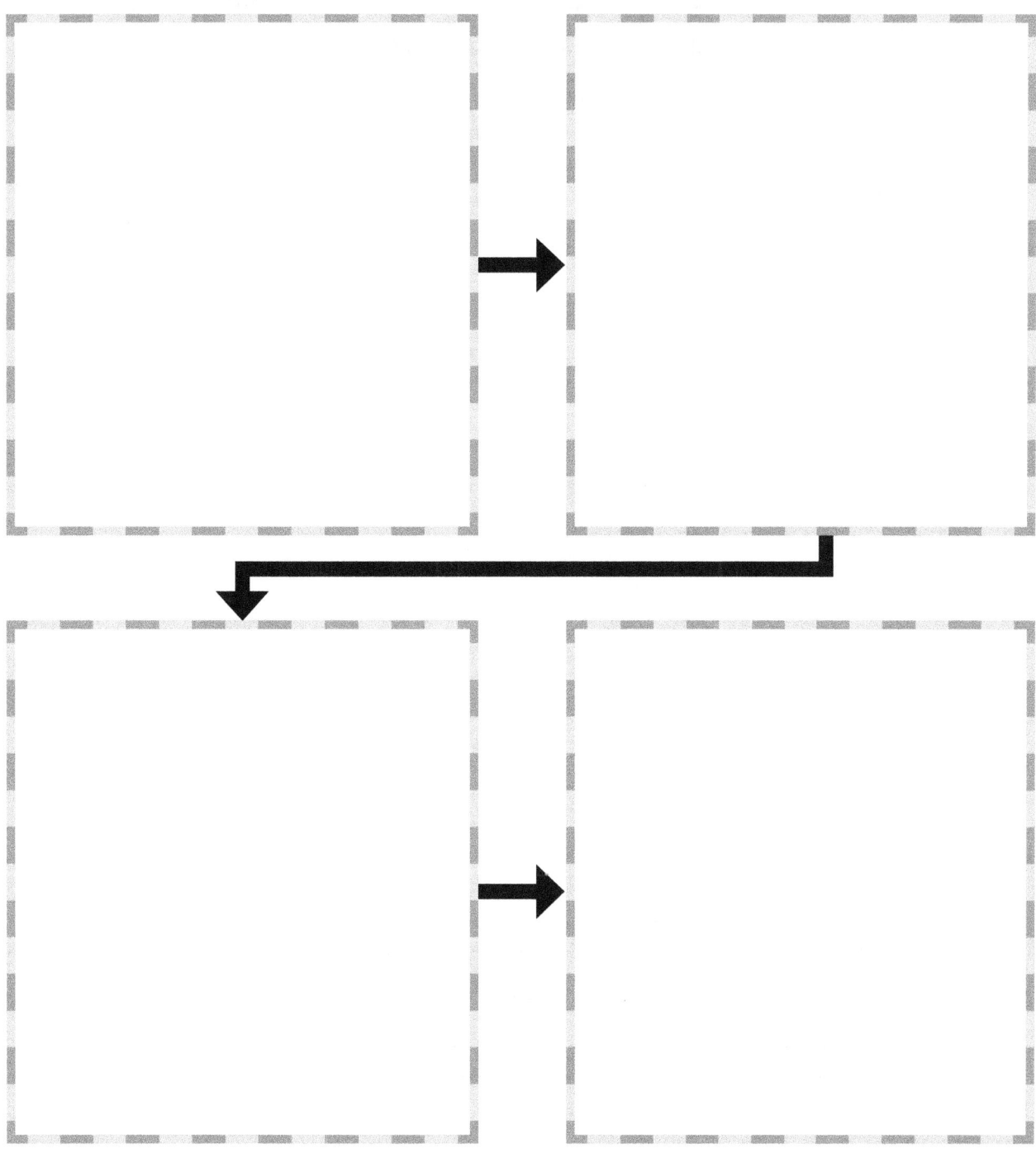

Pages 48–61

Name _____

Story Elements—Character

Directions: The leopard does many things with his spots. He is very proud of his spots. Draw a picture of something special you can do. Write a sentence describing why you are proud of yourself.

Name _____

Post-Reading Activities

Post-Reading Theme Thoughts

Directions: Choose a main character from *Put Me in the Zoo*. Pretend you are that character. Draw a picture of a happy face or a sad face to show how the character would feel about each statement. Then use words to explain your picture.

Character I Chose: _____

Statement	How Does the Character Feel? 😊 ☹	Why Does the Character Feel This Way?
It is okay to be different.		
Everyone is special in his or her own way.		
Things come in all shapes and sizes.		
You can find where you belong.		

Post-Reading Activities

Culminating Activity: The Zoo and the Circus

Directions: Work with students to help them choose one of the following activities. Most likely, these activities will require adult assistance to complete. The puppets on pages 59–61 may be fun for students to use as they perform these different activities.

> Have students create posters that show the leopard as the star of the circus. They should make their posters exciting. The posters should make people want to come to the circus to see the leopard. Students can use crayons or markers. They can even make a collage with lots of pictures!

> Have students work with adults or friends to write reader's theater scripts that retell the book. Students can use the puppets on pages 59–61 for each of the characters. Once their scripts are complete, they can perform their reader's theaters with groups of friends.

> Use the template on pages 62–63 for students to make mini-book retellings of *Put Me in the Zoo*. Make several copies of the second page of the template so the students have many pages in their mini-books. Students will draw pictures to retell the story of *Put Me in the Zoo*. At the bottom of each page, student authors need to write sentences to go along with their pictures. When they finish, they can read their stories to friends.

Culminating Activity:
The Zoo and the Circus (cont.)

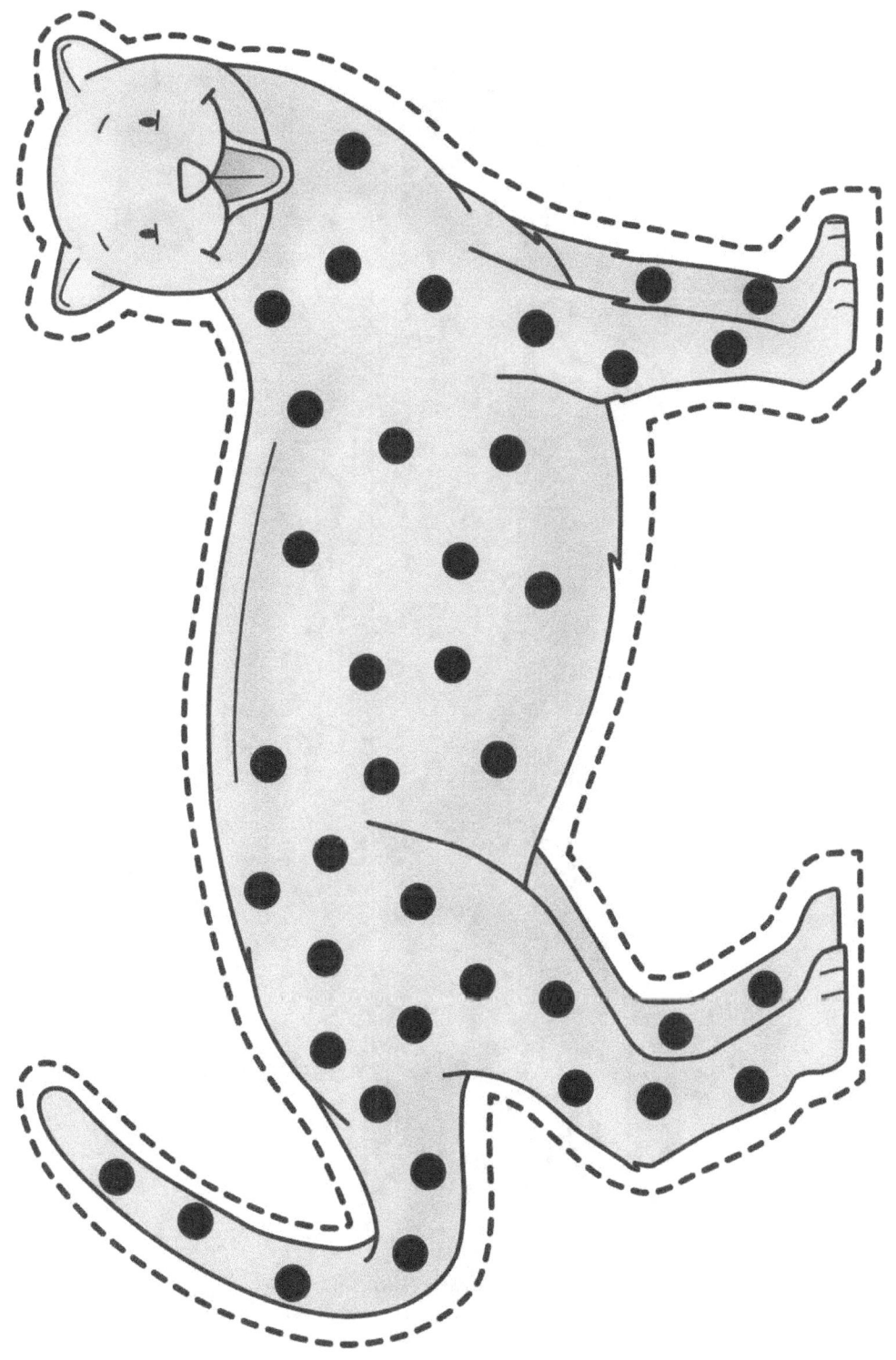

Post-Reading Activities

Culminating Activity:
The Zoo and the Circus (cont.)

Culminating Activity: The Zoo and the Circus (cont.)

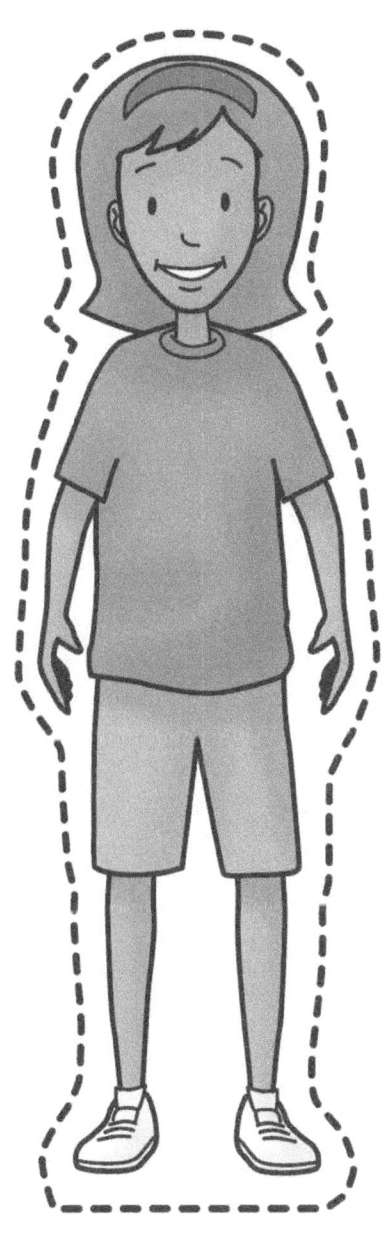
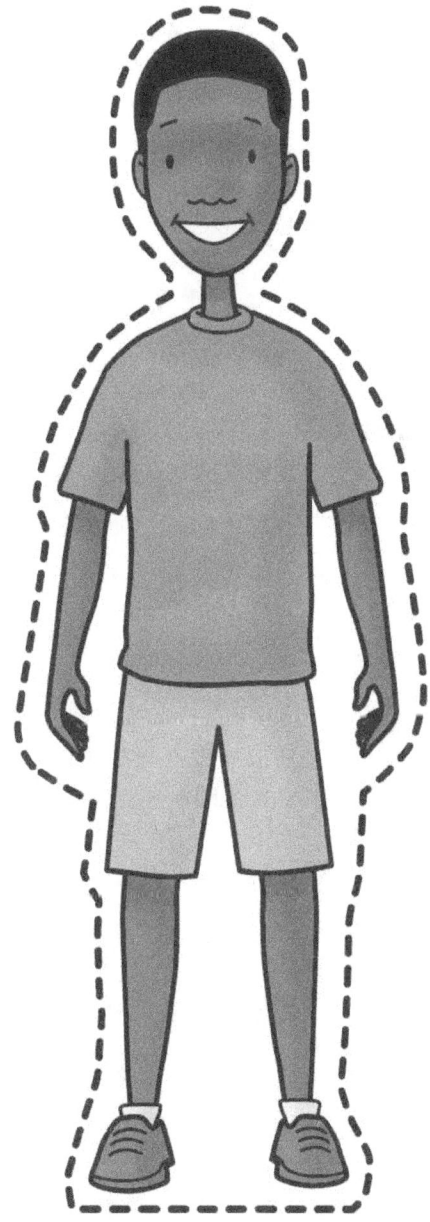

Post-Reading Activities

Culminating Activity:
The Zoo and the Circus (cont.)

Put Me in the Zoo by _____

Page 1

Page 2

Culminating Activity:
The Zoo and the Circus (cont.)

Page ____

Page ____

Post-Reading Activities

Name _____

comprehension Assessment

Directions: Fill in the bubble for the best response to each question.

Section 1

1. What do the zookeepers say to the leopard?
   - Ⓐ "I want to stay."
   - Ⓑ "What good are you?"
   - Ⓒ "Out you go!"
   - Ⓓ "I can do more."

Section 2

2. Where does the leopard NOT put his spots?
   - Ⓐ on a wall
   - Ⓑ on a flower
   - Ⓒ on a cat
   - Ⓓ on a ball

3. Describe some of the places the leopard puts his spots.

   _____
   _____
   _____
   _____
   _____

comprehension Assessment (cont.)

Section 3

4. What does the leopard put his spots inside of?

   - Ⓐ a very tall bench
   - Ⓑ a tree
   - Ⓒ a very small fox
   - Ⓓ a box

Section 4

5. Where does the leopard put his spots right before he goes to the circus?

   - Ⓐ in the air
   - Ⓑ on the wall
   - Ⓒ in a box
   - Ⓓ on the zoo

Post-Reading Activities

Name _____

Response to Literature: The Leopard and His Spots

Directions: The leopard does many things with his spots. Pick your favorite thing he does with the spots. Draw a picture of that scene in a neat and colorful way. Then, use that same scene to answer the questions on the next page.

Name _____

Post-Reading Activities

Response to Literature: The Leopard and His Spots (cont.)

1. What special thing is the leopard doing with his spots?

   _____
   _____
   _____
   _____

2. Why is this your favorite scene?

   _____
   _____
   _____
   _____

3. What happens next in the story?

   _____
   _____
   _____
   _____
   _____

Post-Reading Activities

Name _____

Response to Literature Rubric

Directions: Use this rubric to evaluate student responses.

Great Job	Good Work	Keep Trying
☐ You answered all three questions completely. You included many details.	☐ You answered all three questions.	☐ You did not answer all three questions.
☐ Your handwriting is very neat. There are no spelling errors.	☐ Your handwriting can be neater. There are some spelling errors.	☐ Your handwriting is not very neat. There are many spelling errors.
☐ Your picture is neat and fully colored.	☐ Your picture is neat and some of it is colored.	☐ Your picture is not very neat and/or fully colored.
☐ Creativity is clear in both the picture and the writing.	☐ Creativity is clear in either the picture or the writing.	☐ There is not much creativity in either the picture or the writing.

Teacher Comments: _____

_____

_____

_____

Name _____

Writing Paper 1

Writing Paper 2

Name _____

The responses provided here are just examples of what students may answer. Many accurate responses are possible for the questions throughout this unit.

Vocabulary Activity—Section 1:
Pages 1–23 (page 16)
- After green, he made his spots **violet**.
- All his **spots** are blue!
- What **new** tricks will he do next?
- Will they **keep** me in the **zoo**?
- I want to **stay** in the **zoo**.
1. The children want the leopard to do **more** things with his spots.

Guided Close Reading—Section 1:
Pages 1–23 (page 19)
1. "Why should they put you in the zoo?" "What good are you?" "What can you do?"
2. The leopard turns his spots blue.
3. Students' responses will vary but might include that the leopard looks proud.

Making Connections—Section 1:
Pages 1–23 (page 20)
The habitats will vary, but they should include images and colors that make sense for each animal.

Making Connections—Section 1:
Pages 1–23 (page 21)
The boxes should be colored in as below:
- violet: plum, jelly, may include grapes
- green: may include grapes, shamrocks, grass, frog
- yellow: chick, corn, cheese

Language Learning—Section 1:
Pages 1–23 (page 23)
Students should fill in the blanks with -oo (book, pool, tooth, moon, foot, boot) and draw a picture of each corresponding word.

Story Elements—Section 1:
Pages 1–23 (page 25)
Drawings will vary, but they should show some the following feelings on the leopard's face.
- I want to stay in the zoo.—interested, excited, or happy
- Out you go from the zoo!—sad, disappointed, or confused
- I can make green spots!—proud, happy, or funny
- "Do more!"—amused, happy, excited, or interested

Story Elements—Section 1:
Pages 1–23 (page 26)

 The zookeepers kick the leopard out of the zoo.

 Then, he turns his spots green.

Vocabulary Activity—Section 2:
Pages 24–35 (page 28)
1. The leopard puts his spots **back** on himself.

Guided Close Reading—Section 2:
Pages 24–35 (page 31)
1. The leopard says, "One, two, three."
2. He juggles his four spots as he talks to the children.
3. The leopard thinks he should be put in the zoo because he can do so many special things with his spots.

Making Connections—Section 2:
Pages 24–35 (page 32)
- The *hat* should be circled and written on the line.
- The *ball* should be circled and written on the line.
- The *bug* should be circled and written on the line.
- The *dog* should be circled and written on the line.

Story Elements—Section 2:
Pages 24–35 (page 34)
Students' drawings will vary, but they might include drawings of the spots on a ball, a wall, a cat, a hat, on the zoo, on the children, on a tree, or on the leopard. All the pictures should be labeled.

Answer Key

Story Elements—Section 2:
Pages 24–35 (page 35)
- First: I put my spots on this ball.
- Second: I put my spots on a wall.
- Then: I put my spots on a hat.
- Next: I put my spots on you!
- Lastly: I make four spots.

Vocabulary Activity—Section 3:
Pages 36–47 (page 38)
1. I **take** all my spots.
2. I want to have more **fun**.
3. I can put my spots in a **box**.
4. The spots **look** like **socks**.
5. He makes the spots **small** and **tall**.

Guided Close Reading—Section 3:
Pages 36–47 (page 41)
1. He uses these adjectives: small, tall, and one.
2. These words rhyme: small, all, and tall; fun and one.
3. The leopard has fun making all his spots one. The children are smiling when the spots are small. They seem a bit overwhelmed when the spots are tall.

Making Connections—Section 3:
Pages 36–47 (page 43)
1. **Out** is opposite of **in**.
2. **Noisy** is opposite of **quiet**.
3. **Cold** is opposite of **hot**.
4. **Down** is opposite of **up**.
   - Students' sentences will vary but should use a pair of the antonyms shown.

Language Learning—Section 3:
Pages 36–47 (page 44)
The adjectives should be sorted into the following categories:

Color	Size	Number
blue	big	four
green	small	two
red	tall	one
		three

Story Elements—Section 3:
Pages 36–47 (page 46)
The order of the cards should be:
- The leopard makes the spots very small.
- The leopard makes the spots very tall.
- The leopard puts the spots in a box.
- The spots look like socks.

Vocabulary Activity—Section 4:
Pages 48–61 (page 49)
1. The **circus** is the right **place** for the leopard because he can do so many special things with his spots.

Guided Close Reading—Section 4:
Pages 48–61 (page 52)
1. The leopard asks the children, "Will they put me in the zoo?"
2. The children like all the things the leopard can do. They like his spots, and they like him. However, they do not think he should be in the zoo.
3. She looks very worried or upset.

Making Connections—Section 4:
Pages 48–61 (page 53)
1. 7 + 4 = 11 spots
2. 12 − 6 = 6 spots
3. 9 + 5 = 14; 14 − 2 = 12 spots

Language Learning—Section 4:
Pages 48–61 (page 54)
- The following verbs should be colored in green: fly, see, and call.
- The following nouns should be colored in yellow: tree, circus, two, spot, zoo, and box.

Comprehension Assessment (pages 64–65)
1. C. "Out you go!"
2. B. on a flower
3. The leopard puts his spots on a ball, on a wall, on a cat, and on a hat. He also puts them on the zoo, on the children, on a tree, and even back on himself.
4. D. a box
5. A. in the air

www.ingramcontent.com/pod-product-compliance
Lightning Source LLC
Chambersburg PA
CBHW082246300426
44110CB00039B/2458